BRENTWOOD
INGATESTONE · KELVEDON HATCH

C000172209

Kelvedon Hatch 4 5 Doddinghurst	Ingatestone 3

Coxtie Green 6 Pilgrims Hatch 7	Shenfield 8 9 Hutton
BRENTWOOD 10 Brook Street 11	12 Ingrave 13 Herongate

ROAD MAP   Page 2
INDEX TO STREETS Page 14

Scale of street plans: 4 Inches to 1 Mile (unless otherwise stated)

═══ Motorway	Every effort has been made to verify the accuracy of information in this book but the publishers cannot accept responsibility for expense or loss caused by an error or omission. Information that will be of assistance to the user of the maps will be welcomed.	∿ Stream / River
'A' Road / Dual		Canal
'B' Road / Dual		→ One-way Street
Minor Road / Dual		P Car Park
═══ Track		C Public Convenience
Pedestrianized		🄸 Tourist Information
Railway / Station	The representation on these maps of a road, track or path is no evidence of the existence of a right of way.	✛ Place of Worship
- - - Footpath		● Post Office

Street plans prepared and published by ESTATE PUBLICATIONS, Bridewell House, TENTERDEN, KENT.
The Publishers acknowledge the co-operation of the local authorities
of towns represented in this atlas.

Ordnance Survey® This product includes mapping data licensed from Ordnance Survey®
with the permission of the Controller of Her Majesty's Stationery Office.

A B C D

1

The Grove

Little Hyde Farm

MILL GREEN ROAD
MILL LANE
BACK LANE

LITTLE HYDE LANE

LITTLE HYDE ROAD

BEGGAR

HILL

GREEN ROAD MILL

Fryerning

Playing Field

A12

B1002

BY-PASS ROAD

2

Fryerning Hall

ROAD FRYERNING

FRYERNING

INGATESTONE

School

Willow Green

Willow Green

Kingfishers

New Road

Seymour Field Sports Grnd

Pol Sta

Rays Farm

Cemy

BLACKMORE

DOCKLANDS AV

ROMAN ROAD

3

odds Farm

LANE

BY-PASS

TRIMBLE CL

WADHAM CL

RECTORY CL

Anglo-European Comprehensive School

Wood Lands

CLIFTON TER

HIGH STREET

PINE

PARK

DRIVE

CLOSE

PINE

The HOPPET

DRIVE

STOCK

PEMBERTON AV

VAN STEEN

FRYERNING LANE

MELLOR CL

LASSLER

COURT MWS

P

P

BAKERS

MARKET PL

STAR

THE

SUMMERFIELDS

THE

FAIRFIELD

Ingatestone Junior School

THE MEADS

THE MEADS

MEADS CL

NORTON ROAD

CHAPEL CROFT

CAMERON

DEEP DEAN

STAR LA

POST OFFICE

Fair Field

EYLE CL

FURLONGS

ACRE CL

BARRINGTON CL

Fire Sta

Liby

RD

4

chool

AVENUE ROAD

THE BELVOIR

WAKELIN CHASE

MALTINGS CHASE

CHANTRY DR

STATION LANE

THE ASHLEIGH MWS

IGXTHOUSE MWS

THE PADDOCKS

P

INGATESTONE

WHADDEN CHASE

THE HEYTHROP

THE QUORN

ROMAN ROAD

TOR BRYAN

PETRE CL

HALL LANE

HALL LANE

5

INGATESTONE

Ingatestone Hall

Hotel

THE LEAS CL

TUDOR CL

POPLARS CL

RIDGEWAY

RYE WALK

MARKS CL

River Hey

Heybridge

Bacons Farm

Moat

HALL LANE

6

MOUNTNESSING

A12

BY-PASS

ROMAN ROAD

COURT MDW

MOUNTNEY CL

BURNTHOUSE LANE

QUELOVES LANE

THE HILL WAY

Lodge Wood

Kitchen Wood

A B C D

Stondon Massey

Standon Green

Kelvedon Hatch

Menageria Wood

Courtfield Wood

Clapgate Estate

Picketts Wood

Brook Farm

Round Wood

Kelvedon Grange

Priors Wood

Busby Wood

Willow Tree Farm

Oak Wood

Soaphouse Farm

Mellow Purgess Farm

Pole Wood

Cartshed Wood

The Coppice

Sch

Radio Station

Fish Pond

Church Wood

Playing Field

Pol Sta

Brizes

Place Farm

Furze Wood

Red House Farm

Brizes Wood

ONGAR ROAD

CHIVERS ROAD

NINE ASHES ROAD

SOAMES MEAD

CANNONS MEAD

BRYD MEAD

BLACKMORE RD

CHURCH ROAD

A128

SCHOOL LANE

MILL LANE

EAGLE LANE

KELVEDON LANE

SWAN LANE

FOX HATCH LANE

ROVING DRIVE

GREEN

GLOVERS FIELD

ELMTREE AVENUE

PLACE FARM LANE

STOCKSFIELD

CHURCH LANE

WARREN LANE

DAGWOOD LANE

LUTHERS CL

CHANDLERS WK

THE COPPICE

EAGLE CT

MORRIS

FINCHING FIELDS

WILLOW

HORSEMAN

MATCHING

BARLEY FIELD

BURFF

BRIARWOOD

LYNDALE

SHORT CROFT

BROAD MEADOW

GREAT FOX MEADOW

STOCKS

CL

A · B · C · D

Bentley

Mores
Plantation

The Mores

WARWICK
PL

Pilgrims
Hall

WELL
LA

**Coxtie
Green**

Coxtie Green
Farm

Liby

Sch

Playing Field

ORCHARD LANE

GEORGES DR

VALE CL

ASH CL

PILGRIMS CL

DANBURY
CL

HATCH RO

CROW LA

WILLOW DENE

Larch
Wood

Chestnut
Wood

Shepherds
Spinney

Fox
Wood

Beech Wood

Goldsmith
Wood

Workhouse
Wood

Broom
Wood

The Roughs
Camping Area

Woodland open to public
with nature trails

The Forest

Langtons
Wood

Lodge Field

Foxdown
Wood

Marsh Field

NORTH AVENUE

CHESTNUT AVENUE

Picnic Area

Lake Field

W E A L D   P A R K

Fort

South Weald Lake

Horse Riding Area

C O U N T R Y   P A R K

Recreation
Area

Cafe, Information
& Nature Study Room

Rochetts

Belvedere Field

Brook Weald
Cricket Ground

WEALD ROAD

HOU HATCH LANE

LINCOLNS LANE

COXTIE LANE

MORES

SNAKES HILL LANE

PILGRIMS LANE

GREEN

ASHWELLS ROAD

ASHWELLS

HULLETTS LANE

BELLHOUSE LA

APPLE GATE

ORCHARD LANE

SHEPHERDS LANE

A128

ONGAR

10

A   B   C   D

1

2

3

Shenfield

4

5

6

HALL LANE

HEADS LA

HOME WOOD

BY ROAD

A1023

ROAD

BRENTWOOD

ROMAN ROAD

A12

Six Acre Spring

Arnolds Wood

Shenfield Hall

Hr Wood

Rec Grnd

Grave Yard

Courage Playing Field

Sch

LEWIS

SHENFIELD PLACE

HALL LANE

CHELMSFORD ROAD

HUTTON ROAD

School & Sports Centre

ST MARY'S AV

OLIVER AVENUE

ROCHFORD

HOLMWOOD AV

ALWYNE

AKILWORTH

CROSSWAYS

SEBASTIAN AVENUE

AVENUE

AVENUE

ROAD

LANE

LONG

ALEXANDER

School

Long Ridings

WALTON AVENUE

OAKLAND GDNS

GARDENS

ARNOLD PL

WOODLAND AVENUE

LAUREL CL

RIDINGS

WOODLAND

GRN LONGFORD

HALSTEAD WY

TAXTED

DRIVE

GEO. ROX.

ASHTON CL

PL

ALTHAM GR

POPLAR

BANNISTER

HELMSLEY MEWS

NORMAN PAIGLES

WELL FIELD

WEMM

SHENFIELD GDNS

BOOTHS CT

BIRDBROOK CL

GREAT OAKS

BOWMONT CL

REBBENS CL

Sch

CLAVERING WY

RAYLEIGH

WOTTON CL

YEWTREE CL

THE RETREAT

THE SPINNEY

Fire Brigade H.Q

RAYLEIGH

BYWAY

WESTIN

BARRINGTO

CRESCENT

FARM

LONG FELLOW

TUDOR

SHORTER AV

MARGARET AVENUE

ARDLEIGH

ROCK LEIGH

HUNTER

HIGH ST

Sch

WILLOW CL

PINEL CROFT

JANMEAD

CORY DR

BURSES

SURMAN

NEWMANS DR

DARCY

GREYFRIARS

KINDLE WOOD

Liby

SHENFIELD & HUTTON

Meeting Hall

FRIARS CL

YORK

YORK RD

CL

CLIVEDEN CL

SHENFIELD CRESD PL

HALLWOOD PL

A1023

SHENFIELD ROAD

GLANMEAD

TROTWOOD

GLENDALE CL

MIDDLETON CL

MEAD CL

MILL HILL

MULBERRY HILL

WORRIN ROAD

COOMBE

RISE

ROAD

PARK WAY

PRIESTS LANE

FRIARS LANE

GORDON RD

ABBOTS CLOSE

TYRELL PL

SILVER BIRCHES

PRINCES WAY

HERINGTON GROVE

GREENWAY

ROUNDWOOD

KING FISHER CL

MALLARD WAY

ROUNDWOOD GRO

Roundwood Lake

HUTTON GATE

AVENUE

CHESTNUTS

GROVE

HILLWOOD CL

LONGAFORD WY

CHALLACOMBE CL

Hutton Mount

WIDWORTHY HAYES

WAMBROOK CL

COMPT

LONG MEADOW

HANGING

BROCKLEY

THE GLADE

THE COVERTS

PURBOW WAY

GATEWAY

RIDGEWAY

KILMINGTON CL

To HOSPITAL

Middleton Hall

BRENTWOOD COMMUNITY HOSPITAL

WORRIN

PITWOOD

CRESCENT

DRIVE

WORRIN ROAD

CLANT

THAMS CL

A B A C D

Cricket Ground

School

South Weald

School

Front Park

Vicarage Wood

The Oaks

Weald Brook

Alder Wood

Lower Vicarage Wood

Little Pastures

Post House Hotel

Brook Street

M25 JUNCTION 28

BRENTWOOD

BROOK

Maylands Golf Course

The Grove

Putwell Bridge

COLCHESTER ROAD

A12

Club Ho

Mascalls

M25

Lower Belt

WILLOW WAY
GREEN WAY
KINGREWAY
MAYLANDS WAY
CRAVEN GDS
MOUNT AV

Ingrebourne River

Sewage Works

Boyles Court

HAROLD COURT ROAD

NAGS HEAD LANE

Top Plantation

Boyles Court Farm

Harold Court

Tylers Shaw

WEALD ROAD

WIGLEY ROAD

BUSH

WEALD PARK WAY

BY-PASS

LINK ROAD
BELVEDERE RD
HILLSIDE WALK
WANSFORD CL
TALBROOK
SELWOOD ROAD
BROOK ROAD
SPITAL LANE
THE GROVE
JASON
SHEVON WY
LILLEY
SHEVON WAY
SHEVON DRIVE
WESTBOURNE WY
SOUTHALL WY
MASCALLS GDS
MASCALLS

LONDON ROAD
STREET
HEAD LANE
NAGS HEAD LANE
VICARAGE
A1023
RIVER ROAD
LEONARD WY
WINGRAVE CRES
FERN WY

DARK

A B C D

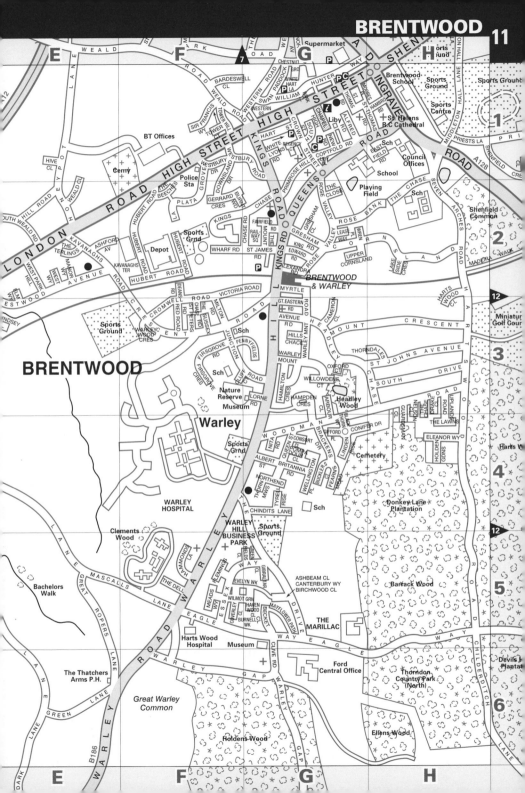

BRENTWOOD

Warley

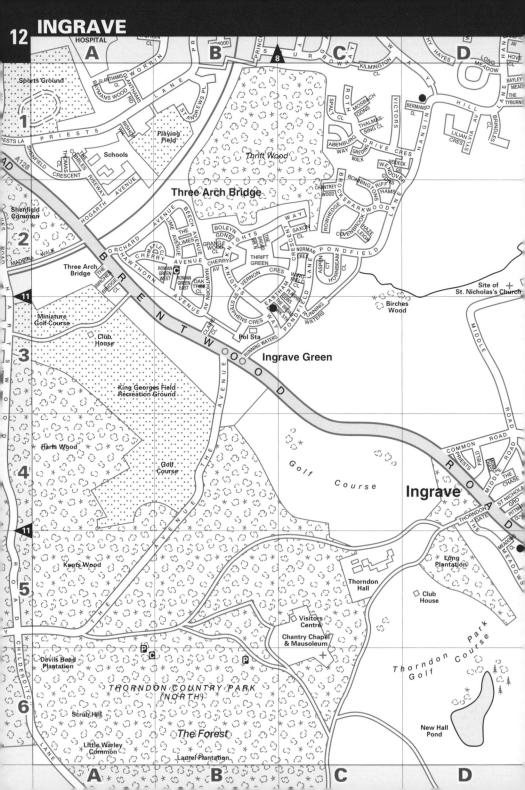